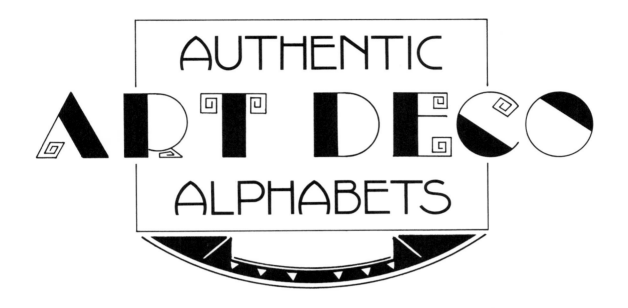

Edited by

LES ÉDITIONS GUÉRINET

DOVER PUBLICATIONS, INC.
New York

Published in Canada by General Publishing Company, Ltd., 30 Lesmill Road, Don Mills, Toronto, Ontario.
Published in the United Kingdom by Constable and Company, Ltd.

Authentic Art Deco Alphabets, first published by Dover Publications, Inc., in 1986, is a new selection of forty-two plates from the portfolio *Publicité - Vignettes - Lettres - Chiffres - Monogrammes et Rehauts Modernes (Modern Advertising, Vignettes, Letters, Numbers, Monograms and Highlights)*, originally published by Les Editions Guérinet, R. Panzani Succ., Paris, n.d. Many of the plates in the original edition were printed in colored ink; in the present edition all the plates are reproduced entirely in black and white. For reasons of design, the linear borders that framed the printed matter on the plates in the original edition have not been retained in this edition. The Publisher's Note and the List of Plates, adapted from the original table of contents, have been prepared specially for the Dover edition.

DOVER *Pictorial Archive* SERIES

Manufactured in the United States of America
Dover Publications, Inc., 31 East 2nd Street, Mineola, N.Y. 11501

Library of Congress Cataloging in Publication Data

Publicité-vignettes-lettres-chiffres-monogrammes et rehauts modernes. English.
  Authentic Art Deco alphabets.

  (Dover pictorial archive series)
  Abridged translation of: Publicité-vignettes-lettres-chiffres-monogrammes et rehauts modernes.
  1. Alphabets. 2. Art deco. I. Editions Guérinet. II. Title. III. Series.
NK3625.A7P813 1986   745.6'197'09042   85-31094
ISBN 0-486-25090-3

PUBLISHER'S NOTE

DURING the 1920s and 30s, a new approach to design came to dominate the decorative arts and architecture in Europe and America. Its name, Art Deco, is derived from the 1925 Paris exhibition L'Exposition Internationale des Arts Décoratifs et Industriels Modernes. The Art Deco movement was a deliberate attempt to create a new style that linked art with the recently established mass-production–based industry. The result was a strongly geometric style, characterized by bold outlines, symmetrical shapes and streamlined, rectilinear forms. One of the style's most enduring expressions was in the distinctive lettering of the period.

Today, the forceful yet elegant look of Art Deco lettering continues to fascinate a new generation of artists and craftspeople. The current revival has led contemporary designers to avidly search out authentic specimens of the abundantly varied Art Deco lettering style. To meet this demand, the present volume, an abridged republication of a loose portfolio of advertising art originally compiled and published by the French firm Les Editions Guérinet, offers a rich assortment of authentic Art Deco numbers, monograms, vignettes, advertising devices and, of course, letters, including fifteen complete alphabets, a rarity in collections of this kind, in which original lettering by advertising artists normally is confined to only a few words for a particular project or advertisement. (There are also eighteen complete sets of numbers.)

As was customary with specimen books of the era, the purpose of the original portfolio was multiple. Not only did Les Editions Guérinet want to show the graphic possibilities of newly created letter and ornamental styles (and the original portfolio was copyright-free just like the present Dover volume), but also to promote the talents of the artists associated with the firm. The forty-two plates in the Dover edition represent the work of four artists, one atelier,

or art studio, and two typographic-design houses, one house being Italian and the other Belgian. When the information is available, the letter and number specimens are identified in the List of Plates that follows this Note, giving the name of the style and the name of the designer.

While an overall cohesiveness—the striking, bold, geometric style—pervades this album and unifies it under the label Art Deco, the work of each of the artists is unique; distinct characteristics are recognizable as being peculiar to each of the artists' styles. Therefore, taking this into account, the plates in the present edition have been arranged in a manner that differs from the order of the original edition. Within three categories, as distinguished in the List of Plates—Alphabets, Letters and Numbers; Monograms; and Vignettes and Advertising Devices—the plates are grouped by artist. The one exception to this is that in the first section the plates are broken down even further, though still grouped by artist within each subsection: complete alphabets are first, several with complete sets of numerals, followed by assorted combinations of letters, some with numbers, followed by two plates of complete sets of numerals.

As you look through this book, it should be remembered that the letter, number and ornamental forms you find here were designed for advertising. Each design is one that might have been used by graphic artists in preparing their layouts, by typographic designers in creating new typefaces or by anyone working in a design situation when the Art Deco movement was at its height. Contemporary artists, designers, craftspeople, printers, typographers, art students and amateurs who seek inspiration and a more intimate acquaintance with the designs of this period are sure to find what they need among these authentic documents of Art Deco lettering, numbering and ornamental work, available copyright-free in *Authentic Art Deco Alphabets*.

LIST OF PLATES

ABCDEF
GHIJKLM
NOPQRS
TUVWXYZ

Plate 1

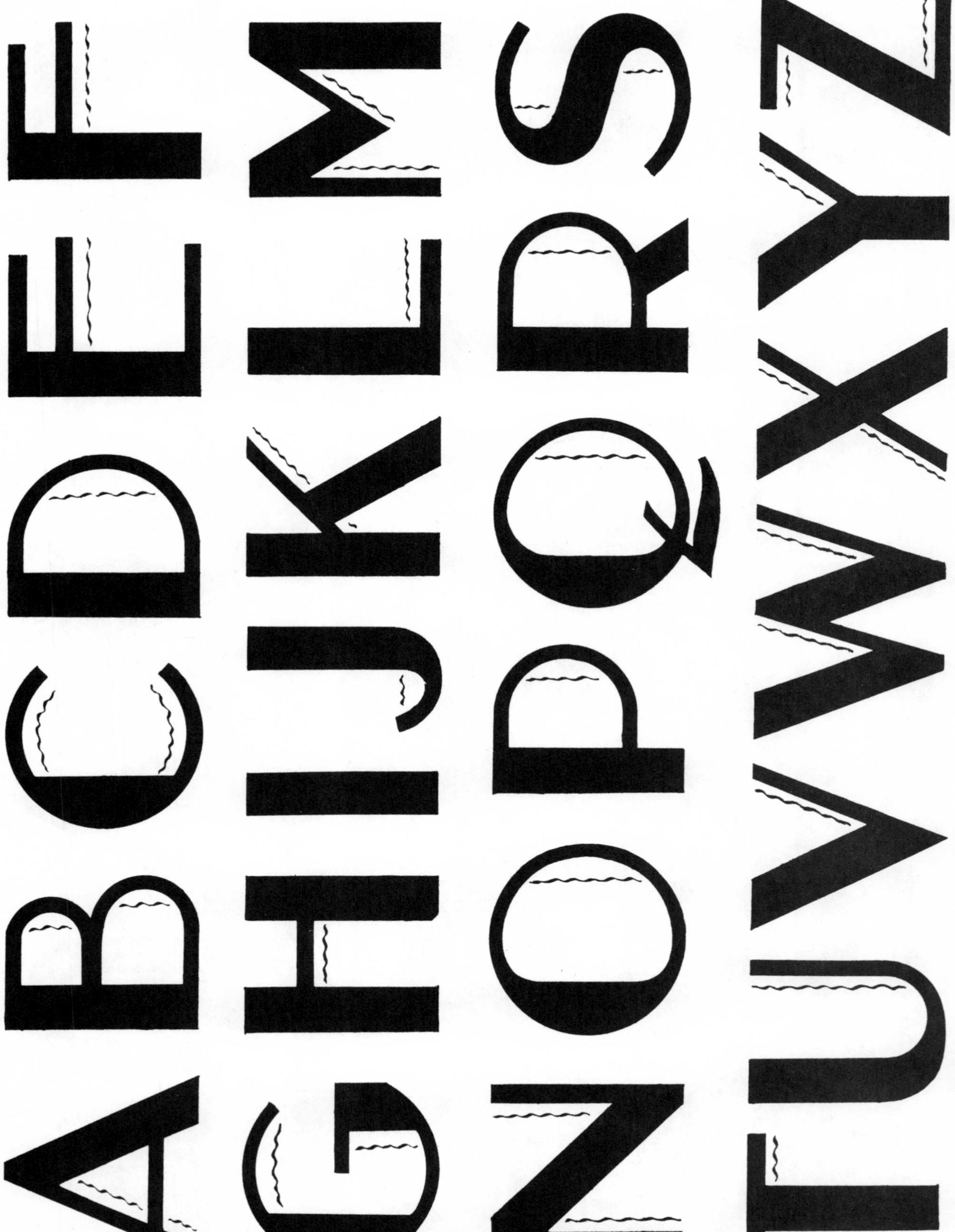

A B C D E F

G H I J K L M

N O P Q R S

T U V W X Y Z

Plate 2

ABCDEF
GHIJKLM
NOPQRS
TUVWXYZ

Plate 3

Plate 4

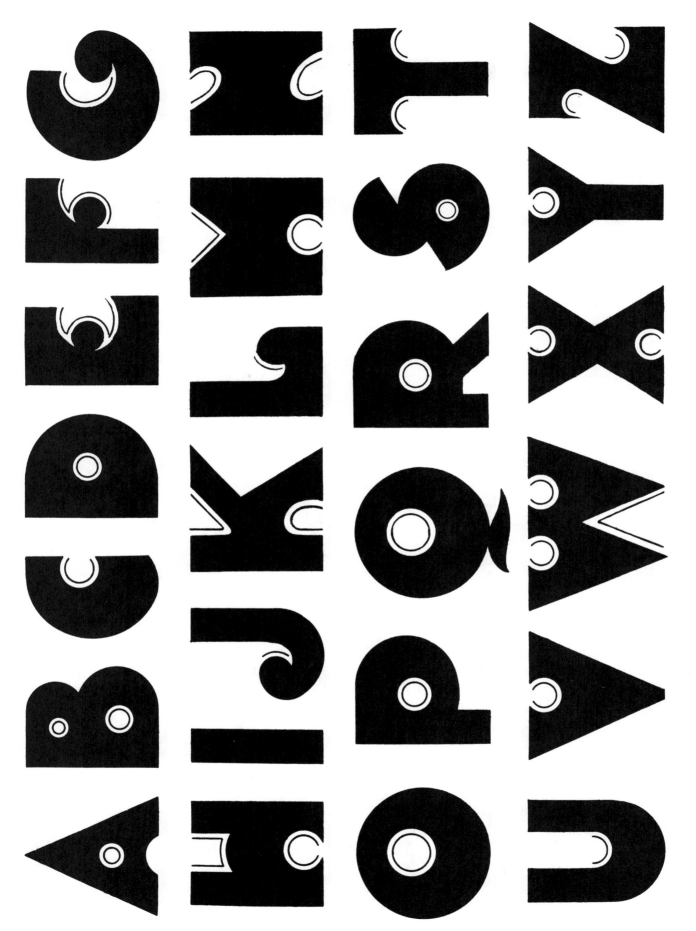

Plate 5

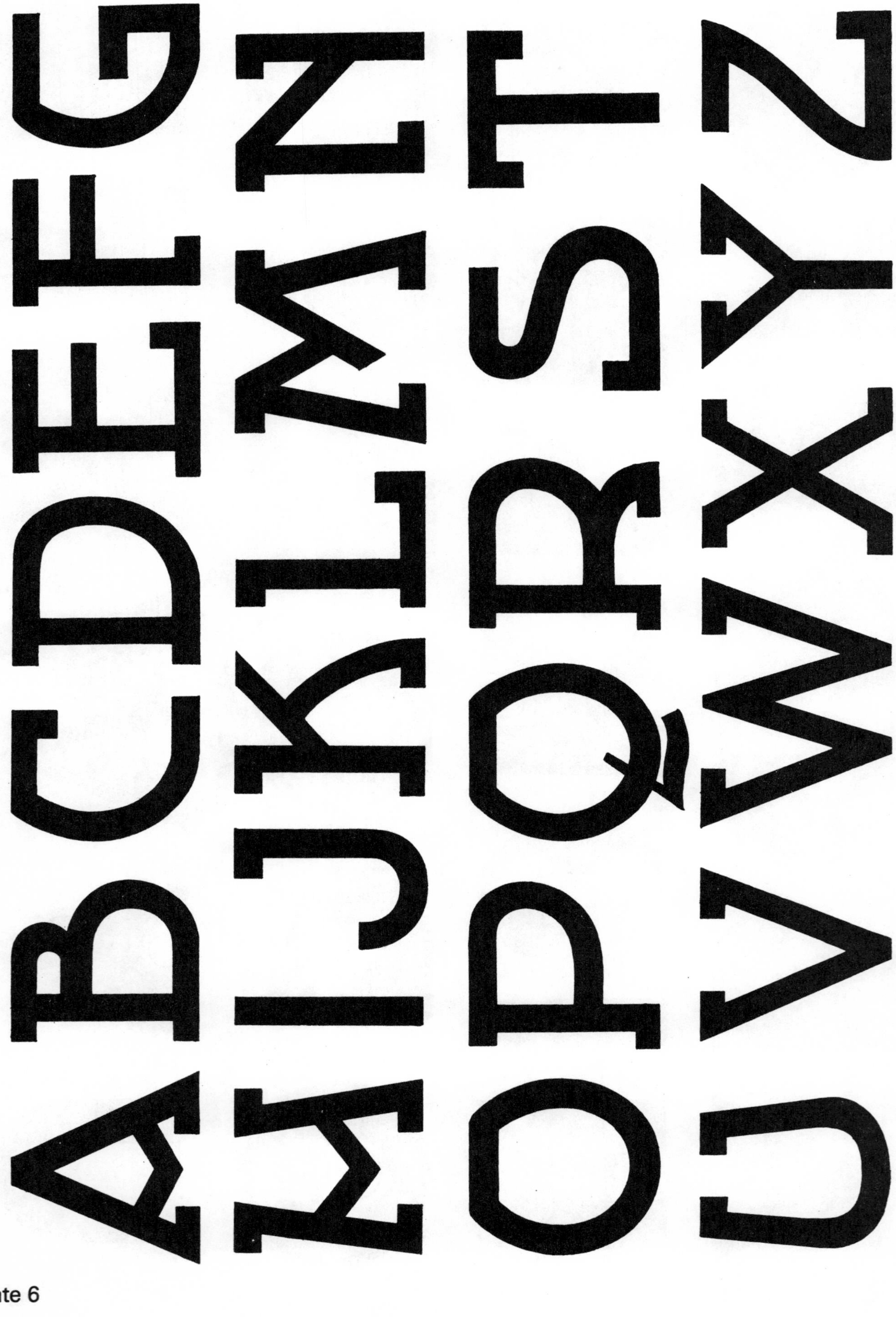

ABCDEFG
HIJKLMN
OPQRST
UVWXYZ

Plate 6

A B C D E F G
H I J K L M N
O P Q R S T
U V W X Y Z

Plate 7

abcdefghijhklmnop

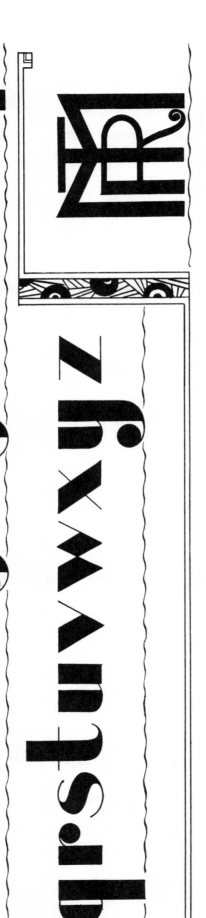

qrstuvvwxyz

ABCDEFGHIJKLMNOPQRSTUVWXYZ

ABCDEFGHIJKLMINOPQRSTUVWXYZ

Plate 8

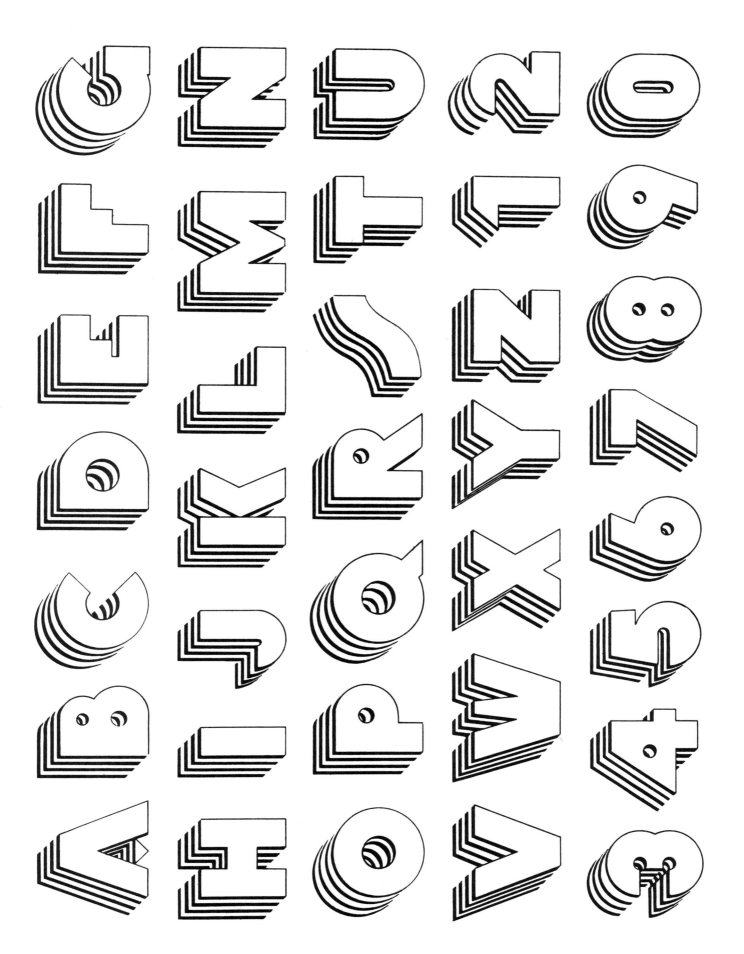

Plate 9

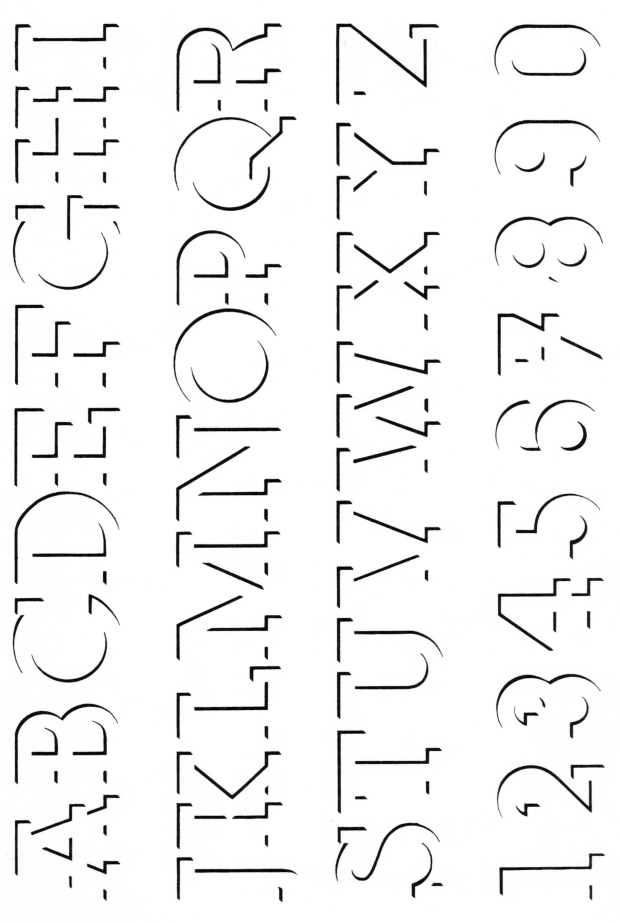

Plate 10

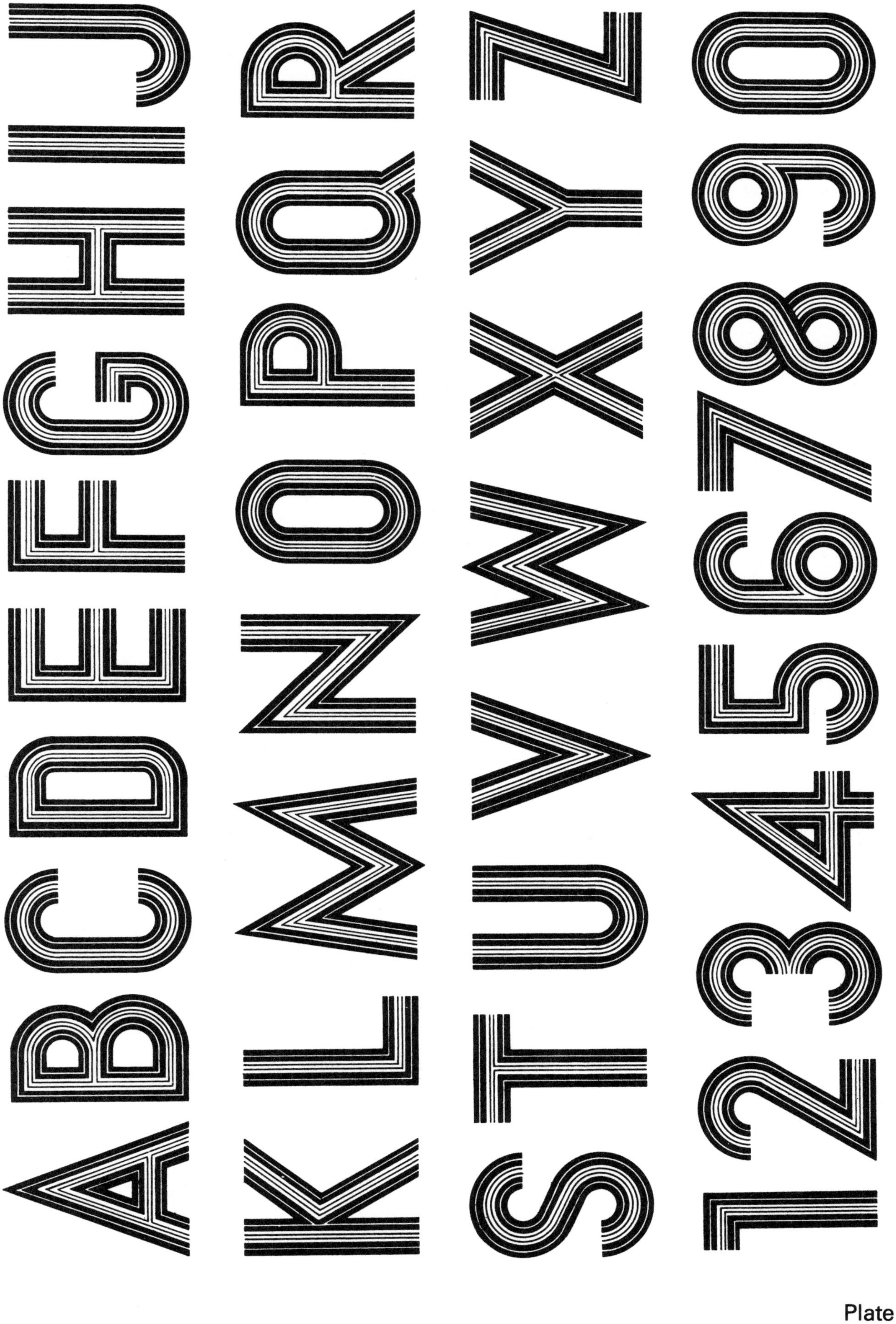

ABCDEFGHIJ
KLMNOPQR
STUVWXYZ
1234567890

Plate 11

ABCDEFGHI
JKLMNOPQR
STUVWXYZ
1234567890

Plate 12

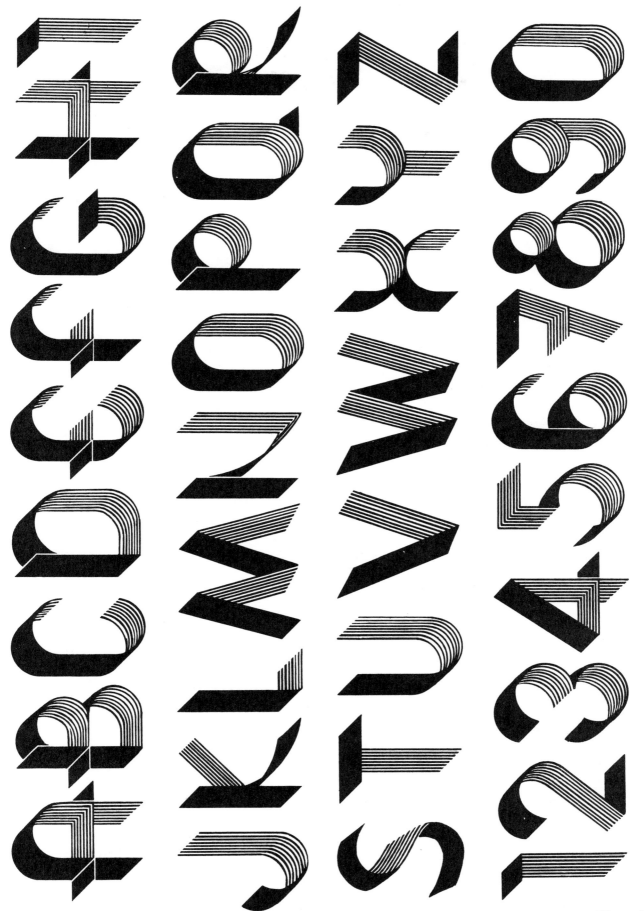

Plate 13

Plate 14

Plate 15

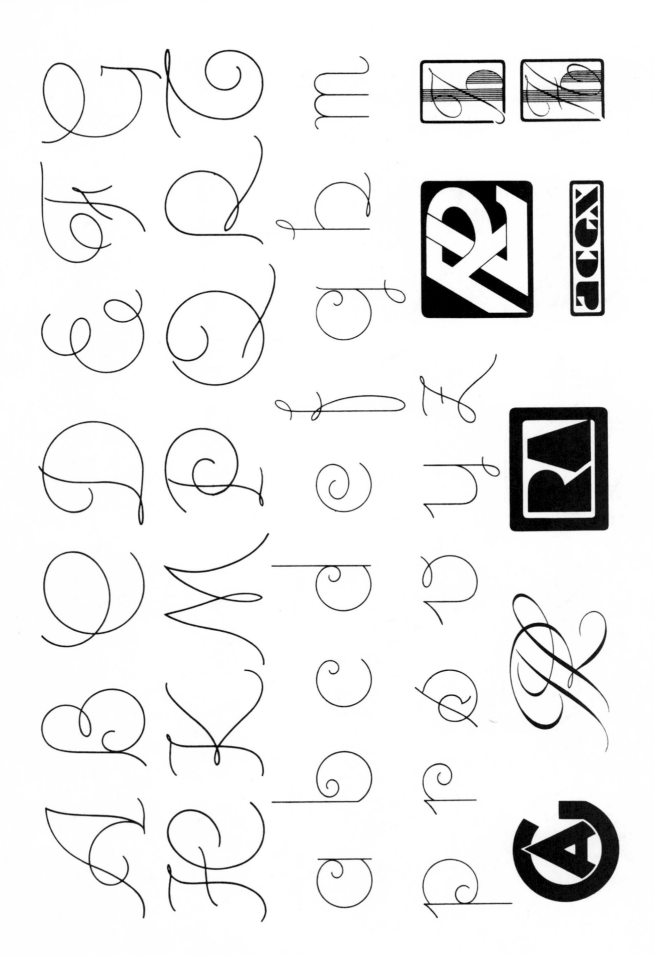

Plate 16

Plate 17

Plate 18

Plate 19

Plate 20

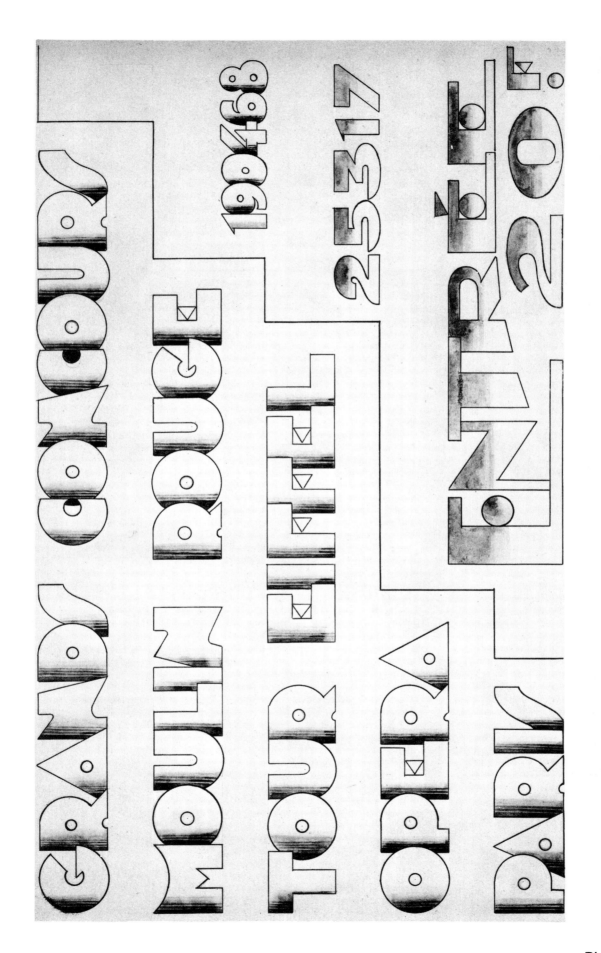

Plate 21

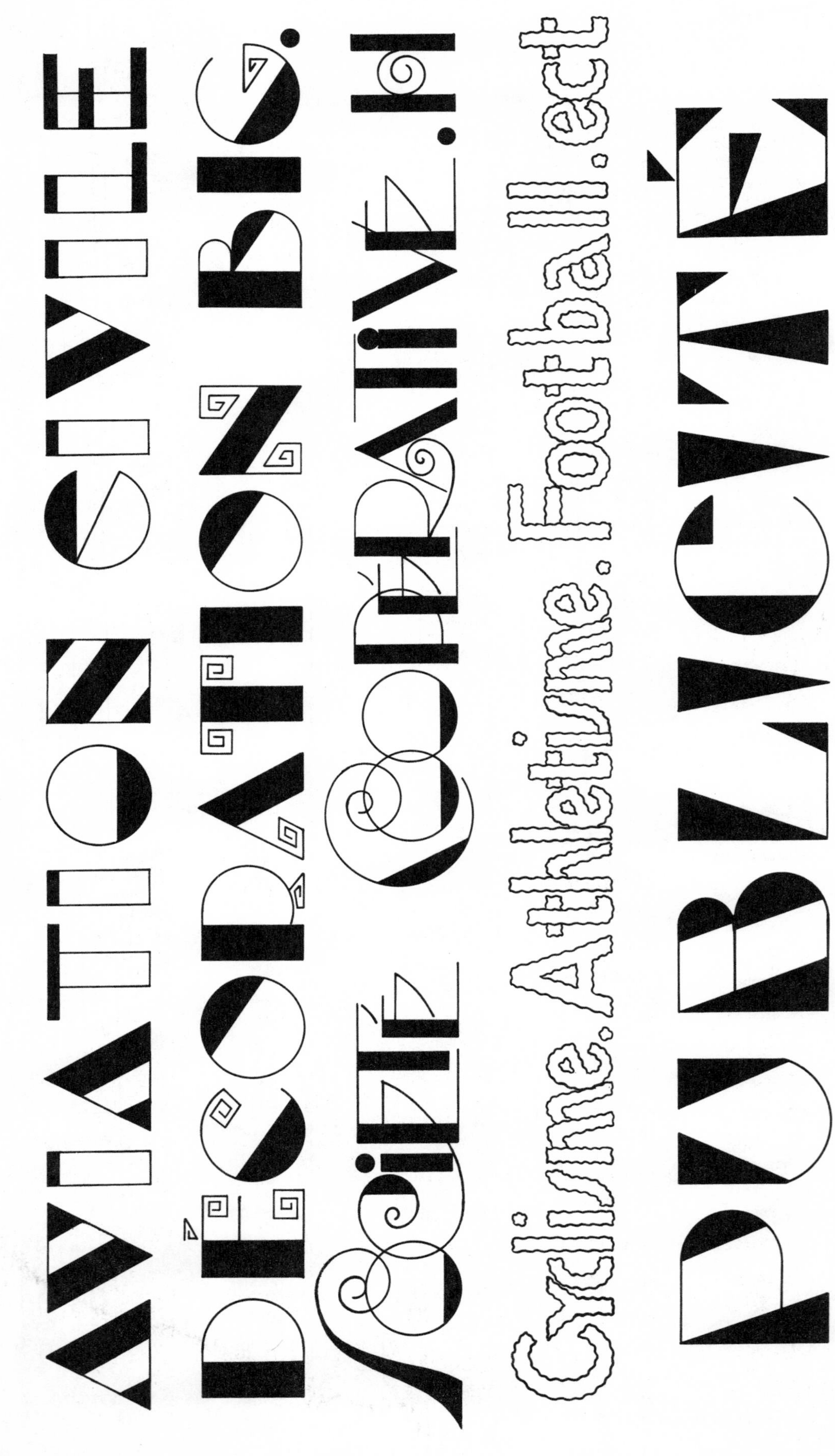

AVIATION CIVILE

DÉCORATION BIG.

Société Coopérative. H

Cyclisme. Athlétisme. Football. ect

PUBLICYTÉ

Plate 22

BOULANGERIE
DISTILLATION
JOINVILLE
Sports-Courses
ILLUSTRATION

BOULANGERIE
DISTILLATION
JOINVILLE
Sports-Courses
ILLUSTRATION

Plate 23

Marco Claudio ebbe dai Romani il
UGOLINO DELLA GHERARDESCA

Banco Comercial de Bernal
DOMINGO DE GUZMAN

NECESSARIAMENTE

INORGANIQUE

REGIONALISTI

MARCONI GUGLIELMO HA
CONSEGUITO DEI GRANDI

PER SAN BENEDETTO
GIUNGE LA RONDINE

SIBILLA CUMEA
I SUOI ORACOLI

RE DI ROMA

BRUMOSO

NERONE

ecco gli araldi, suonan le trombe
e gridano il nome la patria degli

una delle più belle grotte è
la fascinosa grotta azzurra

discendeva il sole in
un magico tramonto

affreschi murali

buona azione

alluminare

allo A. Diaz Duca della Vittoria
\EMORABILI DEL MITE SOLONE

sco Barreto de Meneses
PRINCESA DE LOS URSINOS

Oceano Glaciale Artico
RE DEGLI OSTROGOTI

MONTECASSINO

SIGISMUNDO

DECURIONI

Plate 24

le triste hiver, saison de mort, est le temps du sommeil ou

la leggenda epica non guarda intermezzi di tempi

amore e signoria non soffrono la compagnia

dirección del instituto nacional de Lima

bel paese che appennin parte

COMTESSE DE TONNERRE
GABRIELE D'ANNUNZIO
RENUNCIAMIENTO
ESPRESSIONI
HARMONIE
MESSERI

belle noblesse française

accademia albertina

silenciosamente

numismatico

dimanche

climatici

Plate 25

L'INDÉPENDANT
AFFICHES
PANCARTES ?
UN CARACTÈRE
DE PUBLICITÉ DOIT
ACCROCHER LE REGARD !
UN CARACTÈRE BIEN LISIBLE

Pour vos réclames publicitaires
l'Indépendant reste inégalable

Seul l'Indépendant est le caractère qui
donne toujours satisfaction à vos clients

L'Art Graphique en 1930

Publicité moderne !
Les annonces et
les réclames.

Plate 26

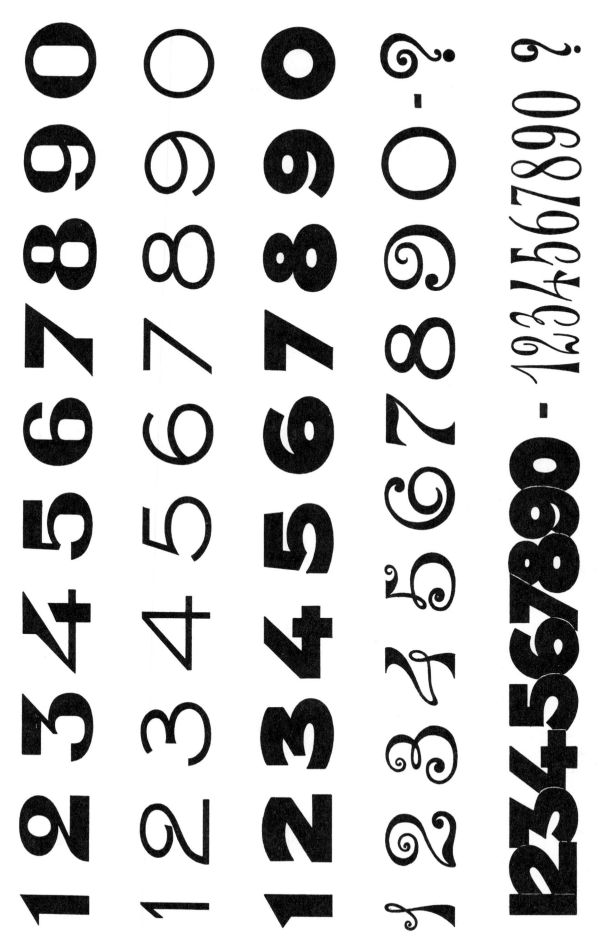

Plate 27

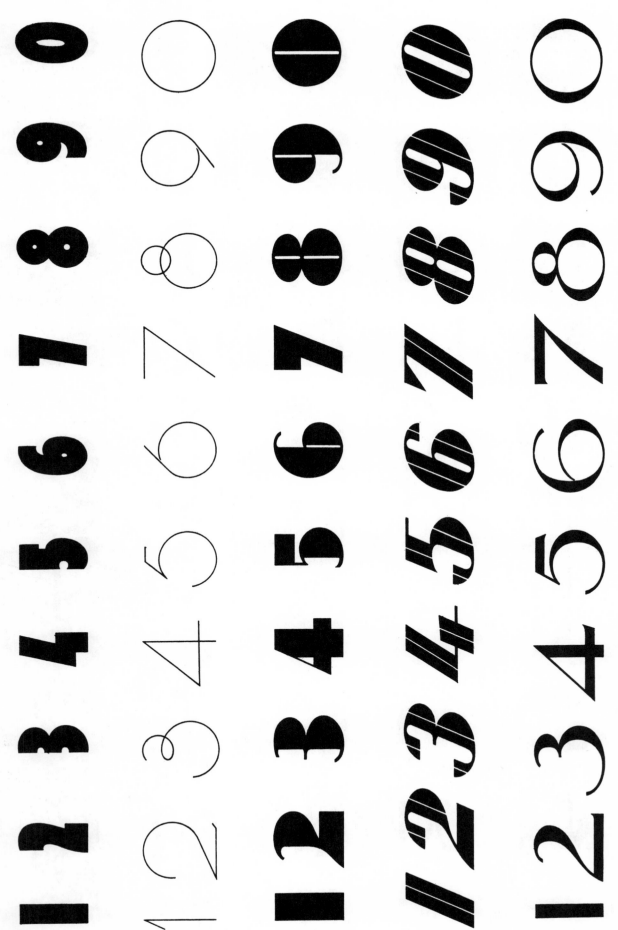

Plate 28

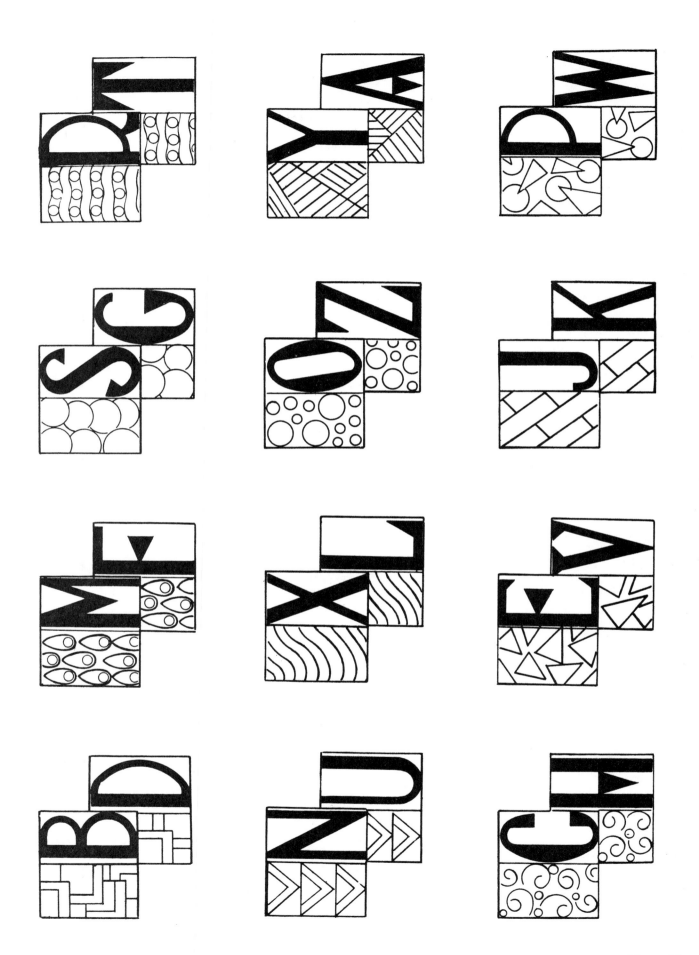

Plate 29

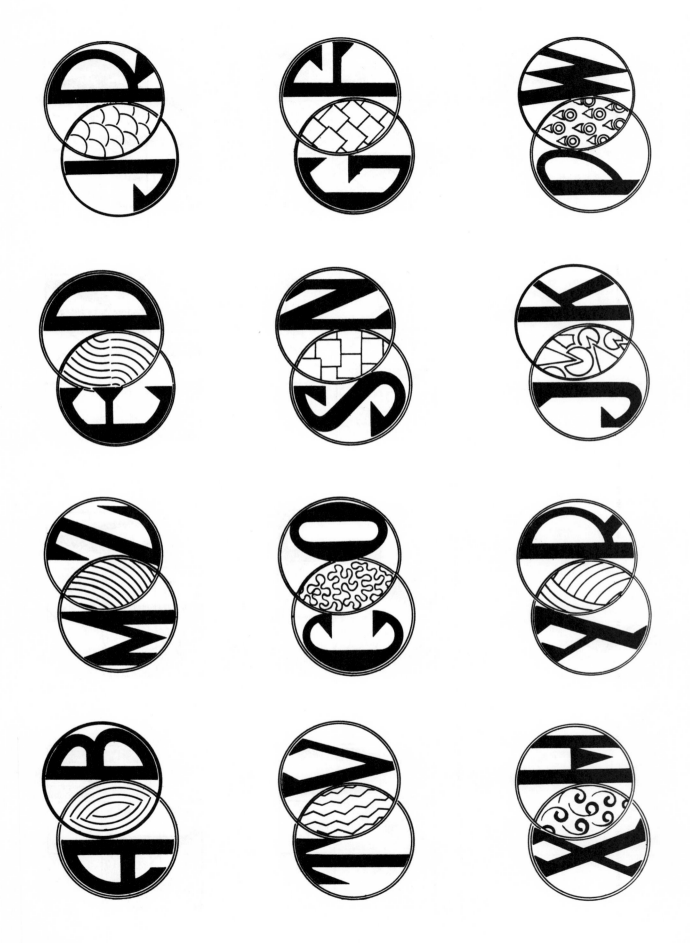

Plate 30

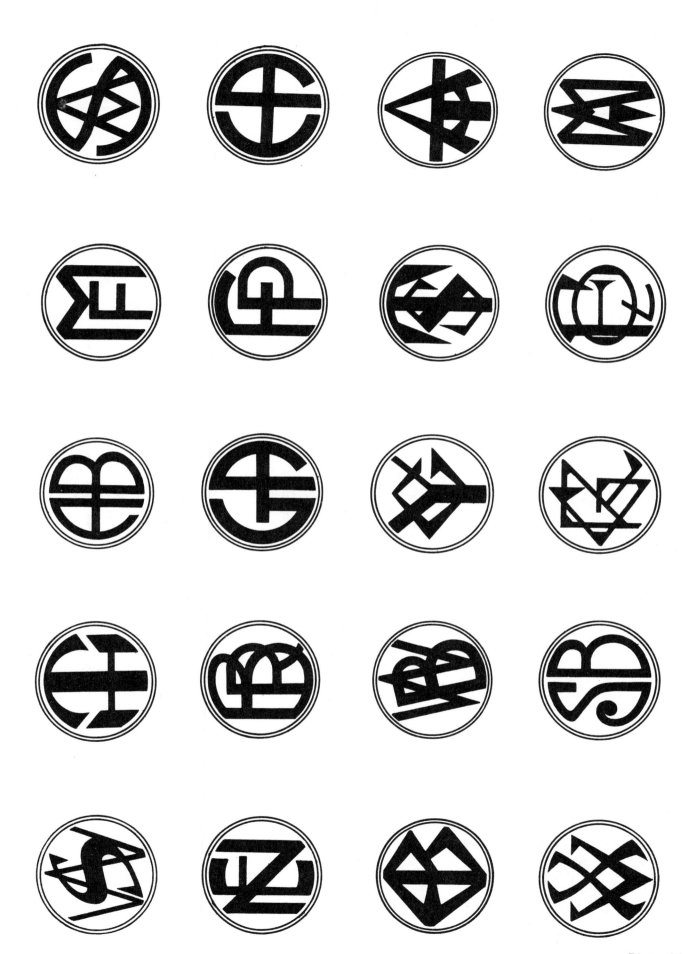

Plate 31

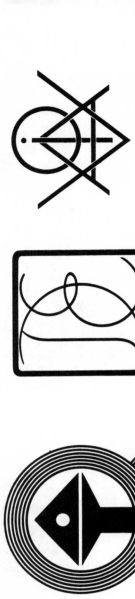

a.J.e.H

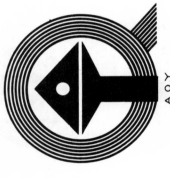

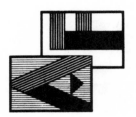

A.Q.Y

P.S.A

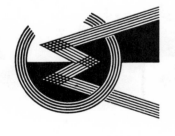

A.E.O.V

O.M

Plate 32

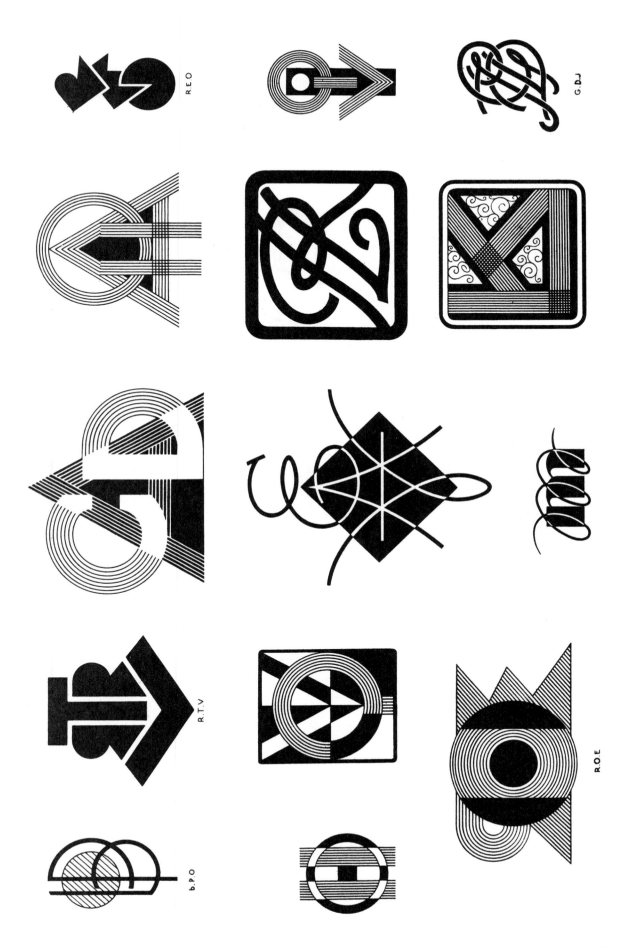

Plate 33

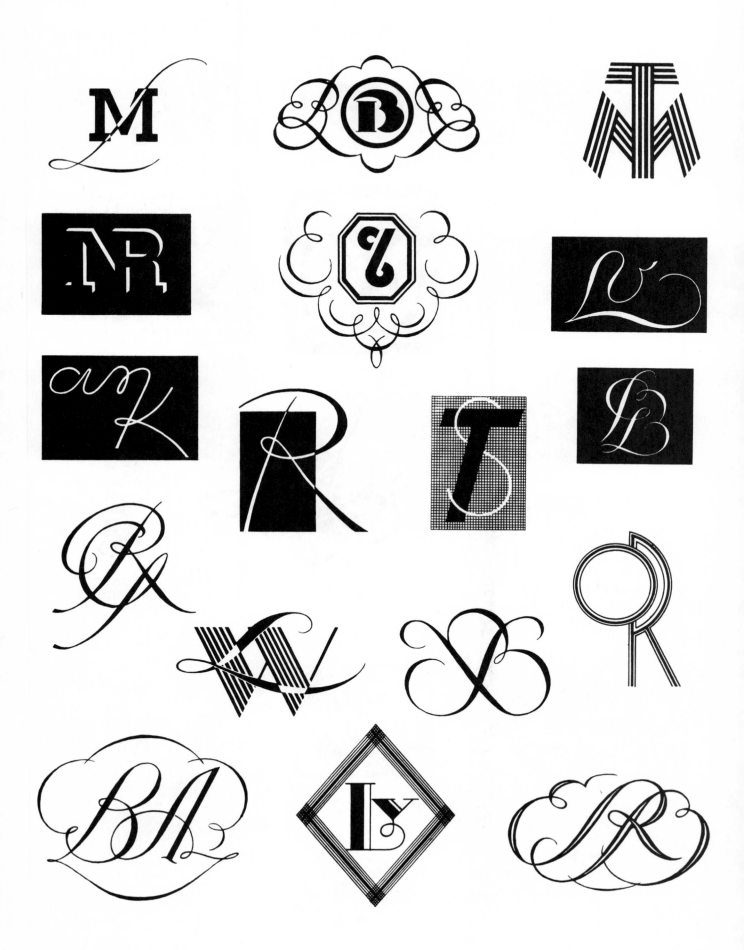

Plate 34

Plate 35

Plate 36

Plate 37

Plate 38

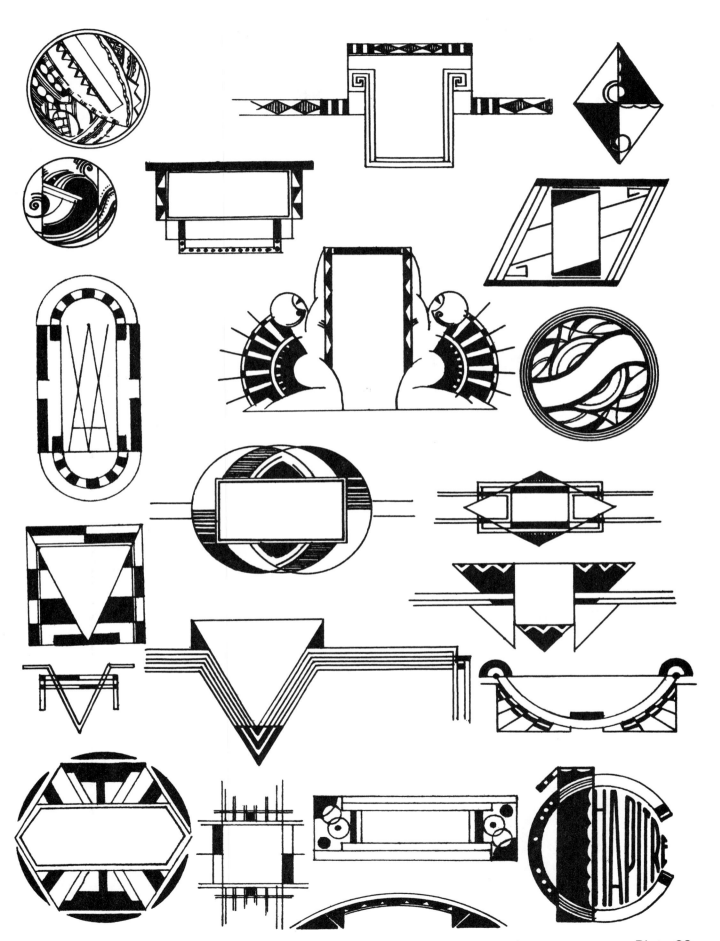

Plate 39

Plate 40

IXE
PARFUMEUR

Plate 41

Plate 42